Author:

Ian Graham studied applied physics at the
City University in London. He then earned a
postgraduate degree in journalism, specializing in
science and technology. Since becoming a freelance
author and journalist, he has written more than one
hundred children's nonfiction books.

Artist:

David Antram was born in Brighton, England,
in 1958. He studied at Eastbourne College of Art
and then worked in advertising for fifteen years
before becoming a full-time artist. He has
illustrated many children's nonfiction books.

Series creator:

David Salariya was born in Dundee, Scotland.
He has illustrated a wide range of books and has
created and designed many new series for
publishers in the UK and overseas. He established
The Salariya Book Company in 1989. He lives in
Brighton with his wife, illustrator Shirley Willis,
and their son Jonathan.

Editor: **Stephen Haynes**

Editorial Assistants:

Mark Williams, Tanya Kant

© The Salariya Book Company Ltd MMVIII

No part of this publication may be reproduced in whole or in
part, or stored in a retrieval system, or transmitted in any form or
by any means, electronic, mechanical, photocopying, recording,
or otherwise, without written permission of the publisher. For
information regarding permission, write to the copyright holder.

Published in Great Britain in 2008 by
The Salariya Book Company Ltd
25 Marlborough Place, Brighton BN1 1UB

ISBN-13: 978-0-531-20702-4 (lib. bdg.)   978-0-531-21912-6 (pbk.)
ISBN-10: 0-531-20702-1 (lib. bdg.)   0-531-21912-7 (pbk.)

All rights reserved.
Published in 2009 in the United States
by Franklin Watts
An imprint of Scholastic Inc.
Published simultaneously in Canada.

A CIP catalog record for this book is available
from the Library of Congress.

Printed and bound in China.
Printed on paper from sustainable sources.

You Wouldn't Want to Be in the First Submarine!

Written by
Ian Graham

Illustrated by
David Antram

Created and designed by
David Salariya

An Undersea Expedition You'd Rather Avoid

Franklin Watts®
An Imprint of Scholastic Inc.
NEW YORK • TORONTO • LONDON • AUCKLAND • SYDNEY
MEXICO CITY • NEW DELHI • HONG KONG
DANBURY, CONNECTICUT

Contents

Introduction

It's 1863. You are an engineer working in a machine shop in Alabama. You build and repair boilers, steam engines, and pipe work of all kinds. You're an expert at any sort of metalwork, but today you are starting work on one of the strangest jobs you've ever done. You're cutting up a water boiler and turning it into a submarine! It's to be called the *H. L. Hunley* after Horace Hunley, one of the men who put up the money to pay for it. Time is short and you'll have to work fast.

The Civil War is raging between the Confederate Army in the South and the Union Army in the North. The Confederacy wants to use the submarine to attack Union warships blockading the South. You can hardly believe men are actually going to dive underwater in it. You're glad you're only building the thing. You really wouldn't want to serve in an early submarine!

Just wait till you see this amazing new invention!

	Union states		Border states
	Confederate states		Western territories

CANADA

MEXICO

Alabama

The First Submarines

The *Hunley* isn't the first submarine ever, but you're hoping it will be the first truly successful one. Drawings and designs for submarines were made in the 16th century. In 1578, Englishman William Bourne designed an underwater rowing boat, but he never built it. The first real submarine was built in the 1620s by Dutch inventor Cornelis Drebbel. It was tested in the River Thames in London. The first American submarine was an egg-shaped craft called the *Turtle*, built in 1775 by David Bushnell. By the 1860s, engineers like you are building submarines out of metal.

ITALIAN ARTIST and engineer Leonardo da Vinci made a drawing of a submarine in 1515, but he didn't actually build it.

Screw

Torpedo

Propeller

Rudder

THE SUBMARINE
Cornelis Drebbel built
in the 1620s may have
looked like this (left).
It was a wooden rowing
boat that was covered with
leather to keep the water
out. Twelve oarsmen
rowed it. One of its dives
is said to have lasted
three hours.

THE *NAUTILUS* (below)
was built by an American
engineer, Robert Fulton,
in 1800. It was covered
with copper. When the
submarine was on the
surface, the crew raised a
sail. Underwater, they
turned a propeller.

THE *TURTLE* submarine (left)
was built for war. It was designed
to be steered up against a ship.
Then a bomb (called a torpedo)
would be screwed into the ship's
hull. The *Turtle* would slip away,
and then the torpedo would
explode. It didn't work.

Cracking the Problems

ngineers like you have been trying for centuries to solve the problems of building submarines. They had to figure out how to make a boat dive underwater. More important, they had to figure out how to bring it up to the surface again! And how do you power a submarine? You could try to find a way of using a steam engine, but it's simpler to get the crew to turn a propeller by hand. When you try this in your workshop, it's easy—you can spin the propeller really fast. But it's much harder to turn it in water because water is so much denser than air.

AIR. The first submarines have no air tanks. The crew has only the air that was in the submarine before it dived. They have to surface before it runs out!

Well, the propeller certainly wor...

LIGHT. It's dark inside an early submarine. Candles provide a dim, flickering light—just enough for the crew to work by.

Handy Hint

Remember to go to the bathroom before getting on the submarine!

DIVING. To dive, a submarine has to become heavier. A valve lets seawater flow into tanks inside the boat, called ballast tanks.

SURFACING. To bring the submarine up again, water has to be forced out of the ballast tanks. It is pumped out by hand—more hard work!

Civil War Submarines

Both sides in the Civil War build submarines to attack each other's warships. The first subs, the Union navy's *Alligator* and the Confederate submarine *Pioneer*, are launched in 1862. The *Alligator* sinks during a storm, after the ship towing the sub is forced to cut it loose. The *Pioneer* is lost to Union forces when they overrun its home port of New Orleans.

Underwater Arms Race

THE *PIONEER* is 34 feet (nearly 10 m) long and made of iron. It's operated by a three-person crew—the captain and two men to turn its propeller.

THE CONFEDERATE NAVY'S *David* steam torpedo boats look like submarines, but they can't go completely underwater.

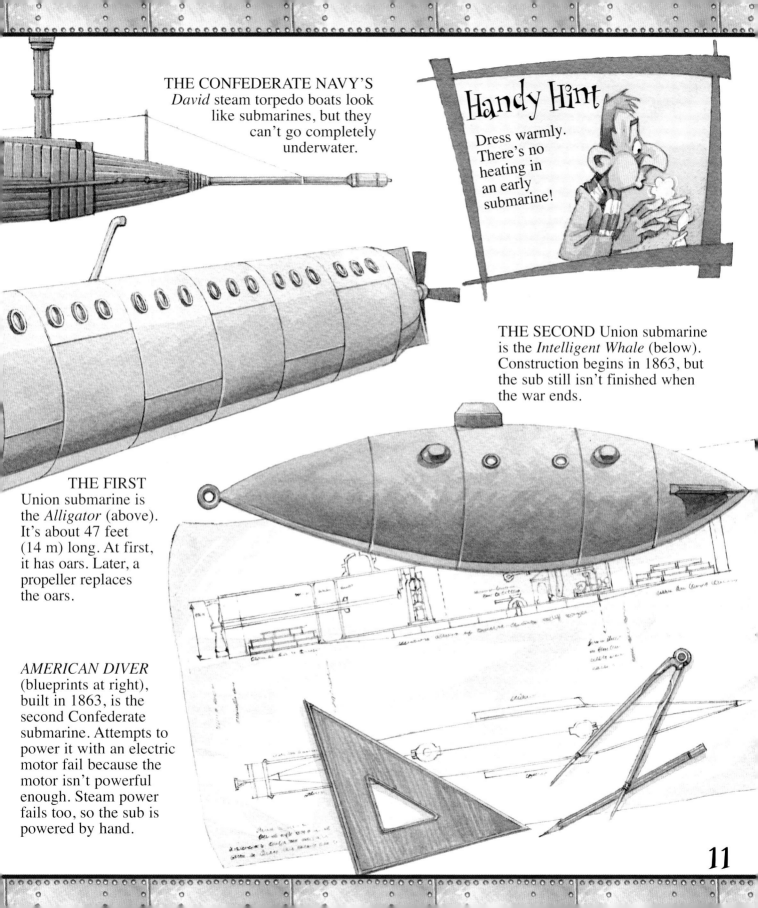

Handy Hint

Dress warmly. There's no heating in an early submarine!

THE SECOND Union submarine is the *Intelligent Whale* (below). Construction begins in 1863, but the sub still isn't finished when the war ends.

THE FIRST Union submarine is the *Alligator* (above). It's about 47 feet (14 m) long. At first, it has oars. Later, a propeller replaces the oars.

AMERICAN DIVER (blueprints at right), built in 1863, is the second Confederate submarine. Attempts to power it with an electric motor fail because the motor isn't powerful enough. Steam power fails too, so the sub is powered by hand.

Mr. Hunley's Submarine

The first stage in building the *H. L. Hunley* is to find a boiler from a steamboat that's about the right size. The one you pick is an iron cylinder about 25 feet (7.6 m) long and 4 feet (1.2 m) across. You cut it in two along its length and insert two flat iron strips 12 inches (30 cm) wide. Then you add a tapering nose and tail. These will help the submarine to slice through the water more easily. Heavy iron plates bolted to the bottom add extra weight to help the sub sink.

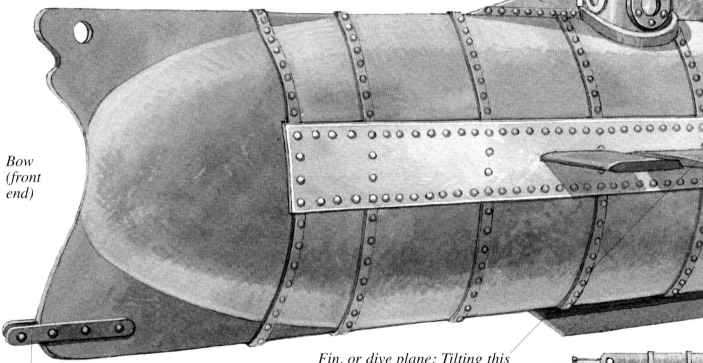

Cutwater: This metal "fin" helps to streamline the entrance/exit hatch.

Forward hatch

Bow (front end)

Spar (pole) for a torpedo (see page 22) is attached here.

Ballast tanks at each end can be filled with water to make the submarine heavier.

Fin, or dive plane: Tilting this down or up helps to make the Hunley dive and resurface.

Rudder: It swivels from side to side to steer the submarine.

Propeller

Aft ballast tank

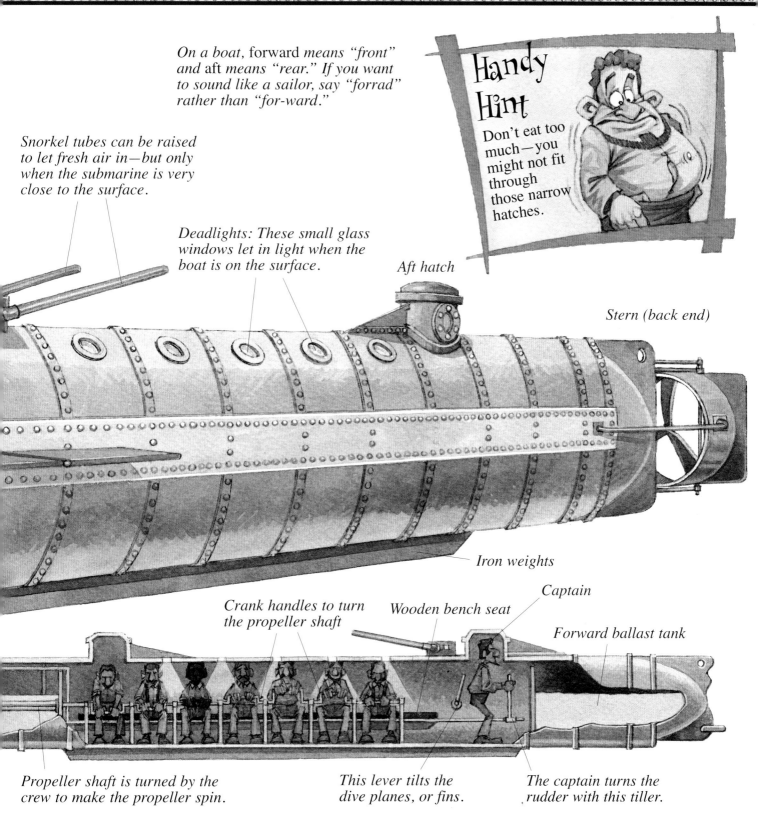

On a boat, forward *means "front"* and aft *means "rear." If you want to sound like a sailor, say "forrad" rather than "for-ward."*

Snorkel tubes can be raised to let fresh air in—but only when the submarine is very close to the surface.

Deadlights: *These small glass windows let in light when the boat is on the surface.*

Aft hatch

Stern (back end)

Handy Hint
Don't eat too much—you might not fit through those narrow hatches.

Iron weights

Crank handles to turn the propeller shaft

Wooden bench seat

Captain

Forward ballast tank

Propeller shaft is turned by the crew to make the propeller spin.

This lever tilts the dive planes, or fins.

The captain turns the rudder with this tiller.

13

Inside the Hunley

Imagine what the *Hunley*'s crew must think of their new craft the first time they see it. Most of them are used to serving on wooden sailing ships. Their new vessel doesn't look much like a warship— or any sort of ship at all! It's a small metal tube that looks as though it's barely able to stay afloat. There are no masts or sails, no decks, and no guns. When the sailors look down into the open hatches, it's pitch-black inside. But now it's time to get on board and practice going to war. One by one, the sailors climb down into the darkness.

Breathe In!

IT'S A SQUEEZE to get into the submarine. The hatches are only 14 inches (35 cm) wide. When you do get inside, there isn't much room. From floor to ceiling, it's about 4 feet (1.2 m) high. Even a child couldn't stand up straight in here!

Maybe I should go on a diet...

And to think I volunteered for this!

That's not a boat—it's a tin can!

Handy Hint

Get in shape, because it's only your muscle power that keeps the sub going.

MAKE SURE you don't bang your head on anything.

ONLY THE CAPTAIN can see outside through small glass ports. He steers with the tiller and dives by using the dive-plane lever.

Diving and Surfacing

TILTING the fins downward makes the sub dive deeper. Water pushes against the fins and forces the sub's nose down.

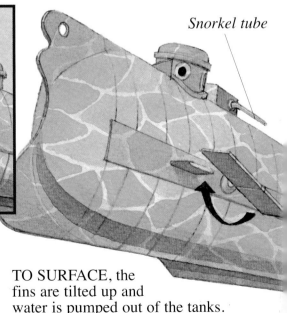

Everyone on the *Hunley* has to work together to make the sub dive safely. While the crew turns the propeller to move the submarine forward, the captain opens a valve called a seacock. This lets seawater flood into the ballast tank in the submarine's nose. The weight of the water makes the nose heavier, and the boat starts to sink. At the same time, a sailor near the stern (back end) of the submarine opens another seacock. This lets water rush into the ballast tank at the stern. Having a ballast tank at each end keeps the submarine level as it dives. To go even deeper, the captain pushes a lever to tilt the fins, or dive planes.

Snorkel tube

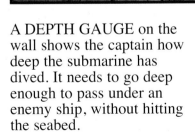

A DEPTH GAUGE on the wall shows the captain how deep the submarine has dived. It needs to go deep enough to pass under an enemy ship, without hitting the seabed.

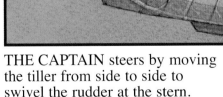

THE CAPTAIN steers by moving the tiller from side to side to swivel the rudder at the stern.

TO SURFACE, the fins are tilted up and water is pumped out of the tanks.

I'm starting to feel out of my depth.

Handy Hint

Don't touch the seacocks unless the captain tells you to. You might sink the sub!

Fresh air can be let in through two snorkel tubes on the top of the submarine, but they have to be lowered before the boat dives. The crew must remember to close the air valves, or water will rush in.

Disaster!

t's August 29, 1863, and the *Hunley* is going on its first mission. Lieutenant John Payne is in command. The crew—all volunteers—are in their seats, and the hatches are open. Lieutenant Payne gives the order to get under way, and the crew starts turning the propeller. As the *Hunley* moves away from the wharf, Payne climbs down through the forward (front) hatch. Immediately, things go wrong. Within seconds, the *Hunley* is heading for the seabed!

What Happened?

1. TANGLED. As Payne climbs into the submarine, he gets tangled in one of the mooring lines that tie it to the wharf.

4. CREW MEMBER Charles Hasker fights his way out of the forward hatch against the flood of water pouring in, but the hatch cover slams down on his leg.

3. LIEUTENANT PAYNE escapes through the forward hatch. Two sailors scramble out of the aft hatch.

2. STRUGGLING to get free, he steps on the dive-plane lever. The submarine's nose dips under the surface, and water pours through the open hatch.

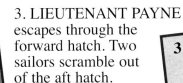

5. THE FORCE of water pressing down on the hatch cover makes it impossible to lift. Hasker is dragged all the way down to the seabed.

Handy Hint

Always make sure the hatches are closed before you start to dive!

6. ESCAPE. The *Hunley* fills up with water. Now the water pressure is the same inside and out. This makes the hatch cover easier to lift, and at last Hasker is able to get his leg free.

7. FREE AT LAST! Hasker is the last person to escape from the submarine. The rest of the crew are drowned.

Disaster Strikes Again

The *Hunley* is raised from the seabed by salvage ships and put back into service. A new volunteer crew is under the command of Captain Horace Hunley himself—the man who helped fund the submarine.

On October 15, 1863, the *Hunley* is practicing how to attack an enemy ship. It heads toward its target—really a friendly ship, the *Indian Chief*—and dives below it. When the submarine surfaces on the other side, a dummy torpedo towed behind it bumps up against the ship's hull. If this were a real attack, the torpedo would explode.

At 9:25 A.M., the *Hunley* sets off for a second practice run.

We'll show them what modern technology can do!

CAPTAIN HUNLEY checks the direction with his compass—once the sub is submerged, he won't be able to see where the target is.

BATTEN DOWN THE HATCHES! The fore and aft hatches are closed and sealed shut. Then the submarine dives below the waves.

SAILORS on the *Indian Chief* watch the submarine dive. Then they rush to the other side of the ship to see it come up again.

Any minute now, boys...

THE SAILORS spot bubbles on the surface, but the submarine never reappears. It has sunk with all its crew. This time there are no survivors.

Oh, no! That doesn't look good.

DIVERS go down and search for the missing submarine. They soon find it sticking out of the seabed with its nose jammed into the mud.

RAISED AGAIN. The divers pass cables under the *Hunley,* and salvage ships pull it up to the surface. Its forward water valve, or seacock, is found open. That's why it sank.

Amazingly, even after these two disasters, people still volunteer to serve on the *Hunley*, and a third crew is soon found.

Final Mission

The third *Hunley* crew tries a new way of attacking—one that doesn't involve diving under the enemy ship. An iron spar, or pole, about 17 feet (5 m) long is fitted to its nose. An explosive torpedo is attached to the spar. The spar has a sharp point so it will stick into a wooden ship's hull. The plan is to ram the spar into the ship's hull and then retreat to a safe distance before exploding the torpedo. On February 17, 1864, the *Hunley* goes into action against a Union warship, USS *Housatonic*.

> Looks like a log, Flemming.

Battle Stations!

BONGGG!!!

CRUNCH

INSIDE THE DARK and cramped *Hunley*, the crew cranks the propeller as fast as they possibly can to pick up speed.

THE PROPELLER turns so fast that it churns up the water and leaves a trail of foaming white waves behind it.

ALARM! As soon as the *Hunley* is spotted, a gong is banged on the *Housatonic* to bring the crew rushing to battle stations.

ON TARGET. The long spar on the *Hunley*'s bow rams into the *Housatonic*'s wooden hull and sticks there.

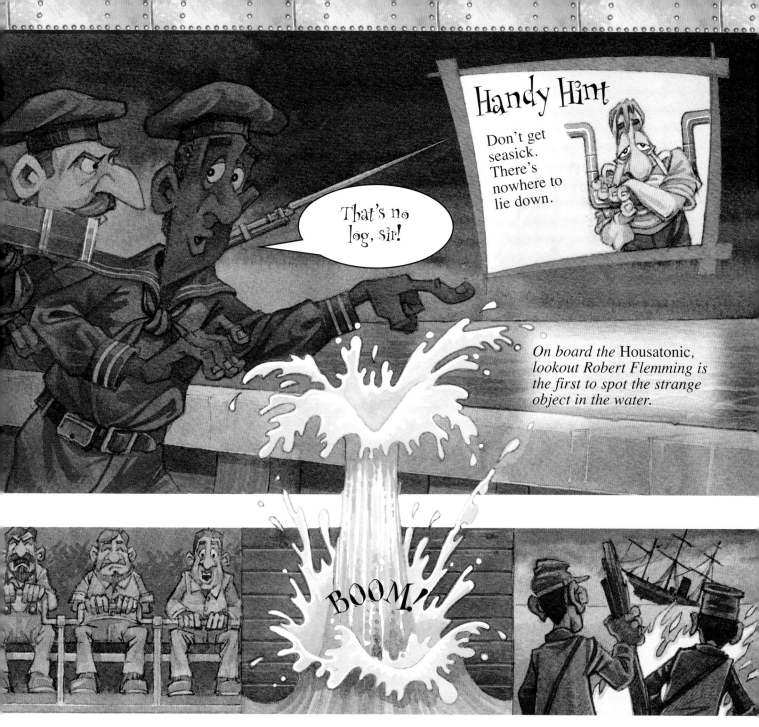

Handy Hint

Don't get seasick. There's nowhere to lie down.

That's no log, sir!

On board the Housatonic, lookout Robert Flemming is the first to spot the strange object in the water.

BOOM!

THE CREW starts cranking the propeller in the opposite direction. As the submarine backs away from the *Housatonic*, a rope attached to the torpedo is pulled, exploding the torpedo.

THE EXPLOSION rips a hole in the *Housatonic*'s hull, and the ship sinks quickly—stern first. The water is shallow, and most of the *Housatonic*'s crew survive by climbing into the rigging.

CONFEDERATE SOLDIERS on shore see a light in the water. Is it a signal from the *Hunley*? The soldiers light a fire to guide the sub home, but it never returns.

23

Finding the Hunley

The *Hunley*'s third crew do not survive their mission, but they have made history: It's the first time that a submarine has attacked and sunk an enemy warship.

After the Civil War ends, various groups try—and fail—to find the *Hunley*. But then in 1995, divers decide to have another look around the wreck of the *Housatonic*. In just over 26 feet (8 m) of water, about 985 feet (300 m) from the *Housatonic*, a diver pushes a pole into the seabed. Three feet down, the pole hits something hard. The diver clears some sediment and feels a curved shape. At first he thinks it's a pipe, but then he feels a hinge. It's a hatch cover! He has found the *Hunley*!

Who Owns the Hunley?

WHEN THE *HUNLEY* is found, someone must decide who it belongs to. The state of South Carolina claims it because the wreck lies off its coast.

THE STATE OF ALABAMA also puts in a claim for the *Hunley* because it was built there. But in the end, neither South Carolina nor Alabama wins its claim.

THE U.S. GOVERNMENT points out that all Confederate property became U.S. government property after the war. The other parties finally agree.

Raise the Hunley!

The *Hunley* is to be raised, but after more than 130 years on the seabed, no one knows how delicate it might be. If it's lifted in the wrong way, it might fall apart. A strong steel frame is specially built for the job. A floating crane lowers the frame carefully until it sits above the *Hunley*. Divers then attach the *Hunley* to the frame with 32 straps. Finally, on August 8, 2000, the floating crane hoists the whole thing to the surface.

THE *HUNLEY* IS OPENED by taking off a panel on the top. The inside of the submarine is filled with fine black sediment.

Steady as she goes!

SCIENTISTS CAREFULLY scrape the sediment away. It smells like rotten eggs! After a few days, they start finding objects belonging to the *Hunley*'s last crew.

Even now that the Hunley *has been raised and studied, scientists still don't know why it sank for the third time.*

THE FINDS include a small medicine bottle, a thimble, a short pencil, and several buttons from the sailors' uniforms.

THE REMAINS of the crewmen are found too. They are buried with full military honors in Charleston, South Carolina, near the graves of other former crewmen of the *Hunley*.

After the Hunley

Back in 1863, when you connected the *Hunley*'s iron plates together, you couldn't help wondering whether submarines had any future. The sub that you built couldn't go very fast and couldn't dive very deep—and it killed most of the people who served on it.

If you could magically come back 140 years later, you'd be amazed by how much submarines have changed. A U.S. *Ohio*-class submarine is a giant vessel, heavier than 2,200 *Hunleys*, and it can dive 40 times deeper.

MODERN SUBMARINES avoid hitting things by using sound. The crew can hear sounds made by nearby vessels. They also send out sound pulses and listen for echoes bouncing back from nearby objects. This is called *sonar*.

YOU WON'T FIND sailors turning a propeller by hand! Today, the most advanced submarines have nuclear engines. The nuclear fuel heats water to make steam. The steam turns a turbine—like wind turning a windmill's sails, but much faster. The spinning turbine drives a generator that makes electricity. The electricity powers a motor, which turns the propeller.

MODERN SUBMARINES don't have to ram a ship to attack it. They fire self-propelled torpedoes that can track their targets.

THE BIGGEST SUBMARINES are armed with rocket-powered missiles that can travel thousands of miles through the air.

Glossary

Aft A sailor's word for "rear."

Ballast Weight that is added to a boat to make it more stable, or to a submarine to make it sink.

Blockade To close off an area to keep people or supplies from moving in or out.

Bow The front end of a boat.

Cable A strong rope.

Cutwater A kind of fin attached to a boat to streamline it, so that the boat slips through the water more easily.

Deadlight A small, thick glass window that does not open.

Depth gauge An instrument for measuring how far beneath the water a submarine is.

Dive plane A fin that can be tilted down or up to make the submarine dive or surface.

Forward (pronounced "forrad") A sailor's word for "front."

Hatch A narrow doorway on a boat. The door itself is called a **hatch cover**.

Nuclear engine An engine that uses the power created by splitting atoms.

Periscope A device that uses mirrors to help you see things that are higher up than you are. Modern submarines have periscopes so that the crew can see what is above the surface.

Port A small round window.

Rigging The ropes and wires on a boat that support and control the sails.

Rudder A hinged flap at the back of a boat that is used for steering.

Salvage To recover a boat or cargo that has been lost at sea.

Seacock A valve that lets seawater into a boat.

Sediment Soft mud that has settled at the bottom of a sea or lake.

Snorkel tube A breathing tube used by divers in shallow water.

Sonar An electronic device that detects objects by sending out sound pulses and listening for the echoes that come back.

Spar A sailor's word for "pole."

Stern The back end of a boat.

Tiller The lever that turns the rudder.

Torpedo An underwater bomb. Modern torpedoes have engines, but early ones did not and had to be towed or pushed.

Turbine A windmill-like machine that can drive an electricity generator.

Valve A seal that can be opened to let water flow or closed to stop it flowing.

Volunteer A person who agrees to do something without being forced to do it. All the sailors on the *Hunley* were volunteers—they served on the sub because they chose to do so.

Wharf A place by the waterside where boats can be tied up for loading or unloading.

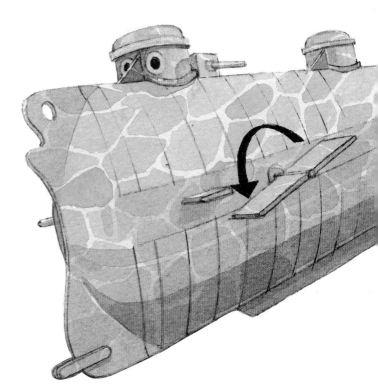

Index